D1686546

Hannah's Revenge
By Juanita Carey

Edited by Nikki Andrews, Kathleen Brandt
and Elena Whiteside

Published by SciArt Media
www.SciArtMedia.com

Hannah's Revenge Copyright © 2010 by Juanita Carey

Front and back cover designs Copyright © 2010 by SciArt Media. Front cover original photo Copyright © 2010 by Andrew Walsh Media. Used with permission.

Inside photos are Copyright © 2010 by Juanita Carey, or are used with permission Copyright © 2010 by their respective photographers, or are believed to be in the public domain, and/or are used for educational purposes under fair use policies.

All stories, content, and text are wholly the work of the author, and does not necessarily reflect the view(s) of SciArt Media.

Front and back cover design by James Maynard and Juanita Carey.

1st Edition first printed April, 2010.

No portion of this book may be reproduced, distributed or adapted for any other purpose without the written consent of the copyright holder(s).

Reviews of Hannah's Revenge

"It's good to read some genuine history, such as Juanita Carey's stimulating *Hannah's Revenge*. A remarkable story, and a remarkable woman, memorialized in Massachusetts and in New Hampshire by statuary, and now in this book."

    Brian Wright
    Coffee Coaster Book Reviews

"To some, Hannah Dustin was a hero; to others a villain... [This is] a new telling of Hannah Dustin's tale..."

    Nancy Bean Foster
    NH Union Leader

"Hannah's intriguing story is recounted with vivid details and images, inviting the reader to envision the historic events."

    Kathe Cussen
    Co-author, *Weather Facts and Fun*

"I loved the book... [T]he story was well written and so appropriate for the elementary students who need to know this story... I couldn't put it down once I started. A great story about a strong woman who did what she had to do for her family."

    Dana G. Crowell
    Library Media Specialist
    Allenstown, NH School District

Table of Contents

Chapter One......... At Home.................... 1

Chapter Two......... The Raid.................... 4

Chapter Three...... The March................. 10

Chapter Four........ The Island................. 15

Chapter Five......... Revenge!.................. 19

Chapter Six........... The Return................ 25

Preface

History is never a one-sided tale. Hannah Dustin is a perfect example of this fact.

I first became interested in Hannah Dustin when I was a school librarian in Allenstown, New Hampshire, responsible for supplying the books teachers needed to enhance their curricula and get kids reading. Fourth-grade teacher Linda Carlisle asked me if I could acquire any books on Hannah Dustin. "She's a very interesting woman in New Hampshire history," Linda told me. Curious, I started looking for any material I could find on this Hannah Dustin. Soon my curiosity changed to frustration.

Books and articles written many years ago, relegated to the quiet depths of the "reserved" New Hampshire History room of the public library, were all that I could find on Hannah Dustin. But as I read them, and Hannah's turbulent times and amazing exploit unfolded before my eyes, I realized that this woman belonged in the front room of the library.

For here was not only a gripping story, but also a very controversial one. I was intrigued by the warm praise and virulent criticism that the very name of Hannah Dustin has generated through the centuries since she lived. Why has she been so loved and so hated? What do our reactions to her tell us about our society and ourselves? And, more importantly, what can today's students learn by looking into the issues from both sides?

Thank you, Linda, for setting me on the trail of this fascinating daughter of her time, Hannah Dustin. Also, I am grateful to all who have assisted me from the beginning of the project to its conclusion. Many have read the manuscript and have offered useful comments. In particular, I want to thank my daughter Kathleen Brandt, an amazing writer and editor in her own right, who gave shape to the story in the beginning and to Elena Whiteside, my good friend and editor, who helped to tighten the manuscript at the very end.

Here is Hannah's story.

CHAPTER ONE - AT HOME

Silently, their tomahawks swinging lightly at their sides, the Indian braves moved through the deep forest in single file. They followed the familiar trails that their ancestors had used for centuries to hunt moose or deer for food, or to trap fox or mink for furs to keep warm through the cold New England winters. But these braves, moving steadily towards the small settlement of Haverhill (in what is now the state of Massachusetts), were on a hunt of a different kind.

They searched for the enemy: the hated white settlers who had relentlessly encroached upon their sacred lands. This raid, like so many before it, had one aim: to capture white women and children and march them north to Canada, where the Indians could sell or barter them to the French, their allies in the bitter struggle against the English colonists.

The year was 1697. The war, now known as the French and Indian War, had been grinding on for many years. Both sides were weary but stubborn. The Indians' tactics of surprise raids and kidnappings had become so successful that every white family in New England had learned to live in dread of them. Survivors, who had been ransomed by their families and returned home, had written about the horrible brutality of the raids and the miseries of the journey north, a forced march of weeks in all kinds of weather with little food or shelter, amid cruel, jeering captors. And although this winter had been quiet – there had been no raids near Haverhill since the previous summer – the colonists knew that every time they looked into the woods the Indians were still there, and could strike at any time.

This particular raid, on March 15th, began like many others. When the Indians came within sight of the settlers' clearings, they split into smaller groups. Hiding behind rocks and trees, staying cautiously away from the sturdy and well-armed garrison houses, the braves searched for outlying farms. These the Indians could attack swiftly and set on fire before disappearing into the woods with their captives – all before help could arrive. Through years of deadly warfare they had become masters of surprise as well as speed.

Although this raid may have begun like all the others, it was not to end like them. One woman, Hannah Dustin, a Haverhill wife and mother who happened to be caught up in the terror of that day, was to transform what had become the settlers' nightmare into her own tale of determination and courage. In so doing she became a legend in her time and the first American woman to be awarded a medal for bravery.

This is her story.

CHAPTER TWO - THE RAID

Cautious and alert, three Indian braves quietly approached a wood-frame house standing by itself in a clearing about a mile outside of the town. Two stories high, it looked solid and prosperous. A cart path led in the direction of the village and a stable, now empty, showed that these settlers owned a horse. Behind the house, outlined by piles of rocks that had been painstakingly removed from the stony ground, was a garden now covered by drifts of snow. No one seemed to be around, but the wary Indians spotted movement behind the windows of the house. They nodded to one another. This was a good target. Keeping alert eyes on the house, they hid themselves behind rocks and trees to wait.

Inside the house, in an upstairs bedroom, Hannah Dustin lay in bed. Six days before, she had given birth to her twelfth child, a baby girl that she and her husband Thomas named Martha. Normally Hannah would be up and around by now, tending to the needs of her large family. In the twenty years since her marriage Hannah had barely missed a day of work. She had helped her husband clear the land and build the house. She had worked alongside him at their farm and brick kiln. She had cooked, cleaned and sewed all the family's clothing. But this birth had been unusually hard on Hannah and Thomas urged her to take a few days rest. The eight surviving Dustin children, ages two to eighteen, all had their chores to do at the farm and a friend and neighbor, Mrs. Mary Neff, had offered to come and help in the house.

"Rest, Hannah," Thomas pleaded. "The children know what to do and can manage without you for a bit. And Mary is here to help as well."

The concern in his eyes settled the question for Hannah. Life in their wilderness was hard indeed; the Dustins had suffered the loss of three children already. Hannah was well aware that without her it would go very hard for Thomas and the children. And so she rested.

Meanwhile, out in the woods, the braves watched the house. Seeing that all was quiet, no one approaching along the path, they nodded once more to one another. The time was now.

Inside, peace at last descended after the bustle of getting the family off to their morning work. Mary Neff, downstairs in the kitchen at the back of the house, started the noonday meal. Hannah remained upstairs with the baby.

Suddenly, the morning stillness was shattered by ear-splitting gunshots and the shrieks of war-hoops.

Hannah's first thought: hide baby Martha under the bed. But before she could do anything more than throw a blanket on her, the low doorway was filled by an Indian brave brandishing a tomahawk menacingly in her face. He was decked in buckskins and feathers and his face was covered in war paint. In panic, Hannah cried out as he grabbed her roughly by the shoulders and pushed her in front of him down the stairs and out to the snowy clearing. Clasping her baby tightly against her chest, gasping, stumbling, bruising her bare feet on the frozen ground, Hannah was driven towards the woods, hugging her precious burden.

Two other braves in war paint appeared from behind the house. One carried a sack of looted household goods while the other pushed a trembling Mary Neff. Behind them, flames engulfed Hannah's beloved home. She heard gunshots resounding from the direction of Haverhill. In agony, all Hannah could think about was her family. Where, oh where, was Thomas? Where, where the children?

But there was little time to dwell on what might have happened. As the Indians pushed them hurriedly beyond the village and out into the dark forest, it was all Hannah could do to keep her balance on the icy trails and not fall with the baby in her arms. After a while they came to a small clearing where other hostages stood huddled in a group, an Indian brave standing guard over them, tomahawk at the ready. Other Indians seemed to be conferring with one another. But Hannah's eyes went straight to the prisoners where, in shock, she recognized neighbors and friends, ten in all. Neither Thomas nor any of the children were among them. Quietly, with dread, she asked what had happened in Haverhill and was told they had seen twenty-seven killed – men, women and children.

"Do you know anything about Thomas, or my children?" she asked again and again of the captives. But no one had an answer.

It wasn't long before the Indians, their brief council ended, strode forcefully towards the shivering group, motioning them with raised tomahawks towards the woods. The captives clung to one another in fear. Baby Martha began to cry.

Up to now, huddled against her mother's breast and in constant motion, the baby had been quiet. Now, however, standing still in the blustery cold and feeling the tension all around her, the infant's pitiful wailing rose, echoing through the surrounding trees. In desperation, Hannah shushed her daughter. She jiggled her up and down as they began to move forward, impatient braves always at their heels.

They had not traveled more than half a mile when one of the women, a friend of Hannah's who had been having trouble keeping up the swift pace, stumbled and fell on the trail. Hannah stared dumbly at her, unable to help because of the baby in her arms while others rushed to give her a hand. Before they could reach her, one of the Indian braves, his face expressionless, strode over to the woman and struck a swift blow to her head with his tomahawk. The woman lay still, her blood flowing over the frozen ground.

For a moment all was silent, the captives too stunned to say a word. Suddenly, one of them began to scream hysterically. Startled, baby Martha began to cry again, this time louder than before.

One of the braves strode towards the captives, tomahawk raised again. The screaming woman stopped suddenly but once Martha had started crying there seemed nothing that Hannah could do to quiet her. As the Indian came near her, she backed away, holding the baby in one arm while she stretched out the other to fend off the enemy. From the corner of her eye she could see Mary Neff reaching out as if to take the innocent baby she had so often held over the past six days but the Indian could not be stopped. With one swift, cruel motion he seized the tiny bundle from Hannah's grasp and flung it hard against a tree.

Baby Martha fell silent, her crying hushed forever.

Groaning, Hannah sank to the ground. She didn't care if the Indians killed her; she had no more will to live. But Mary and the others hurriedly pulled her to her feet, urging her to keep going. They half-pulled, half-carried her as the group was forced to take to the trail again, trudging through the wintry forest. And, in time, Hannah's aching heart realized that they were right. She must go on. She must stay alive for Thomas and the other children. But were Thomas and the other children even alive?

CHAPTER THREE - THE MARCH

For the next ten days, pushed and prodded by their cruel enemy, the little band of hostages marched north through the woods. They slept at night on the frozen earth and ate what berries and roots they could find. Occasionally the Indians threw some maize or dried venison at them and, stifling their bitter resentment, the prisoners ate it. For Hannah the journey was an agony that even in her later years she never forgot. With no baby to nurse, the milk swelled painfully in her breasts, reminding her daily and hourly of her cruel loss. Although the Indians had tossed her a pair of shoes from their store of loot Hannah's feet were so frostbitten and bruised that every step she took was torture. And even worse than the physical suffering, uncertainty about the fate of her beloved family overwhelmed her thoughts.

She remembered that the children were to go to the farm and Thomas had said he was working at the brick kiln. Could he have gotten to them in time?

Could they have possibly made it to the safety of the garrison house? Hannah was tormented by the thought that the children would have been alone and defenseless when the Indians had come so suddenly. Somehow she *must* get back to find out what happened to them. How, she did not know, but with every step that took her farther from her home, Hannah Dustin swore that somehow, someday she would return.

Occasionally, during their brief periods of rest, Hannah shared her worries about Thomas and the children with Mary Neff. But they always came up with the same question: how could their ragged band, cold, hungry and weaponless as they were, find a way to escape from this well-armed and organized foe?

One day, as they trudged ever northward, Hannah was overtaken on the trail by one of the Indians. He came close and began to speak to her in a low voice. To her amazement, she realized that this young Indian was speaking English. "So sorry, Ma'am, about the baby. I feel for your pain." Hannah, her eyes growing wider, stared at him. It took a moment before she realized that this young man was not an Indian at all, but a white boy who looked like them because he was wearing Indian clothing.

"Who, who are you?" she managed to whisper hurriedly, still staring at this unlikely sight.

"I'm Samuel Leonardson, Ma'am." He spoke in a rush. "I grew up in Worcester. My family is there - I hope. But I have been with this band for a long time, at least a year that I can count. I can hardly remember. I thought long ago that they would sell me up north, but here I am. At first they were cruel and fed me little, but after a while they seemed to get used to me and I have made friends, in a way, with some of the braves. I can now speak a bit of their language; they seemed to think that funny and so I've stayed. I've learned some things from them as well." He paused and took a breath. "I hate what they did to your baby. How could they do that? I want to go home. I don't even know what has happened to my family."

As she listened in amazement to this young man, Hannah's curiosity was piqued. "What have you learned from them?" she asked.

Samuel glanced around him again to see if any of the Indians were watching or listening. He lowered his voice. "Well, one of the braves showed me how to kill someone instantly, and how to take a scalp. I've never done it," he hastened to add, "but I would if I had to – to get back home."

Mary Neff, who had been listening silently to this conversation, trembled. Hannah kept silent. She was thinking.

After ten grueling days on the trail, the Indians halted in a spot in the woods where they joined other Indians, including women and children. A heated discussion ensued between the braves, while the squaws stood on the side and the children chased one another in play.

During those days the band of Haverhill captives had decreased considerably. Twice more during the journey a few had fallen to the ground and been killed instantly by their impatient captors. Now, as Hannah listened intently to a discussion she could not understand, it seemed to her that they might be divided into even smaller groups. When the bartering and exchange of beads and rifles was complete, Hannah and Mary were handed over to a small band of Indians consisting of only two braves, three women and seven children. To her intense relief, Hannah saw that her new friend Samuel was also in their group.

As they headed off into the woods, Hannah looked over her shoulder at her fellow Haverhill townspeople herded in a different direction. With a heavy heart she realized that she might never see them again. But as she walked quickly next to Samuel and Mary, Hannah was also thinking of something else. She was remembering Samuel's words: *"I've never killed anyone, but I would if I had to — to get back home."*

Hannah Dustin didn't know if she had a home left. She didn't know if her husband and children were alive, or if they had been massacred. But one thing she did know as she marched north. Come what may, she would return to Haverhill to find out.

The statue of Hannah Dustin in Boscawen, New Hampshire.
Photo by Juanita Carey.

CHAPTER FOUR - THE ISLAND

For the next fifteen days Hannah, Mary and Samuel trudged north with their new band of captors. If Hannah had thought that it would be easier to escape from this smaller group, she soon found that she was mistaken. To make up for fewer braves, the squaws carried tomahawks as well. And although they were given more food, the captives were watched constantly. Any movement one of them might make towards the woods, away from the group, would bring a loud squawk from one of the children. Then a brave or squaw would come running towards them, shouting angrily in their language, with a tomahawk raised threateningly in the air. Hannah realized that if she were going to escape, she would have to learn to be like her foes. She would have to watch and wait for the perfect moment.

As the days passed, Hannah found herself helping Mary more and more, encouraging her when it would have been so easy for the older woman to give up. Whereas it had once been Mary who had kept her alive after the death of baby Martha, now Hannah provided the help when the trail got especially rough. Now Hannah pressed her to eat to keep her strength. All the while she watched and waited, thinking of Samuel's words: *"I've never killed anyone, but I would if I had to — to get back home."*

One day, almost a month after the raid in Haverhill, the Indians halted at a spot on the bank of the Merrimack River. Here they took several canoes from hiding places in the underbrush. They bundled Hannah, Mary and Samuel into them, and paddled swiftly north with their captives. For the first time since the raid Hannah was able to rest her weary limbs. Yet as she sat in the canoe, watching the trees along the shoreline glide quickly by, she knew that she was moving north more swiftly than ever.

But then another thought occurred to her. If one paddled downstream, *with* the current rather than *against* it, one could quickly make up for lost territory. If she and Mary and Samuel could only steal a canoe, they would be able to move south much more quickly than on foot.

Late that afternoon the Indians arrived at their destination: a small island in the junction of the Merrimack and Contoocook Rivers, near what is today the city of Concord, New Hampshire. It was a beautiful little island, about two and a half acres in size and covered in dense forest. Bluffs rose from the beach, providing a perfect lookout on all sides.

As she stretched her cramped limbs, Hannah saw trails leading up the bluffs to whatever was at the top. It seemed to her that this island must be the place where Indians stopped on their long trek north. After beaching the canoes the Indians scrambled up the bluffs pushing the captives before them. At the top, Hannah and the others saw a flat clearing, with woods all around. There the squaws and children began gathering wood and soon a large fire was burning in the center of the clearing.

"They've built a big fire. They must feel safe here," Hannah thought as she sat just outside the ring of Indians. Could that help her to form a plan?

Soon the squaws had cooked a meal and the Indians ate with a good deal of laughter and shoving. It was obvious that they were celebrating, either that they had successfully eluded the whites, or that the end of their long journey to Canada was close at hand. Hannah felt a clutch of fear. She knew that there was little time left. If she were going to act, it would have to be soon.

Before long the braves and children nodded off in sleep. The squaws, after finishing their chores, checked that their captives were sleeping. Then they too lay down and were soon slumbering.

But not all the captives were asleep. Although Hannah's eyes were tightly shut, she was awake and alert. As she lay beside Mary and Samuel she kept a wary eye on the group by the campfire. She was watching and waiting for the perfect moment.

The island now known as Dustin Island, where Hannah, Mary, Samuel and their captors rested for the night.

Photo by Juanita Carey

This is the house where Thomas and the children hid after the attack.
It is now called the Duston Garrison House and it is in
Haverhill, Massachusetts.
Notice the different spelling of Hannah's last name.
Photo by Juanita Carey.

The night of the escape, pictured in a painting from 1847, by Junius Brutus Stearns.
Public domain image.

Hannah and her group escaping from the island.
Public domain image.

The marker at the site of the home of John Lovewell, whose home Hannah stayed at after her escape, on her way back home to Haverhill.
Photo by James P. Walsh II and www.jcbwalsh.com. Used with permission.

Plaques in Haverhill, Massachusetts chronicle the journey of Hannah Dustin. Above: Thomas and the children escape from the attack. Below: Hannah and Mary Neff are led away.

Above: The night of the attack on their captors. Below: The escape back to Haverhill.
Photos by Tara Leystra. Used with permission.

The statue of Hannah Dustin in Haverhill, Mass.
Photo by Juanita Carey.

CHAPTER FIVE - REVENGE!

About midnight, Hannah silently rose. She put her finger over her lips to quiet Samuel and Mary, who had awakened from a light slumber and were watching her intently. Cautiously she tiptoed over to the group by the campfire. She walked around the silent sleepers, gently prodding them with her foot to see if any woke up. But they stirred not a muscle. Hannah stood back and took a deep breath. Her heart was pounding wildly, but her head was cooler than she would ever have thought possible. She knew what she had to do, and she knew that finally the moment had come.

Now she was the one who held the advantage of surprise. Now she could strike her enemy unawares. She could never get back baby Martha's life, but she could avenge it. Even more importantly, she could take back her own freedom, and Mary and Samuel's as well. Then she could get back to Haverhill, and finally find out what happened to Thomas and the children.

Hannah saw the Indians' tomahawks, lying where they had thrown them down. She tiptoed over to them. Taking a tomahawk in her own hands, she turned to Mary and Samuel, who had risen and followed her. Not a word was said between them as they held each other's eyes. Samuel and Mary each picked up a weapon from the ground. He handled it with confidence, having seen one used many times. But Mary, trembling all over, could barely keep hers in her grasp.

Hannah walked swiftly over to a sleeping brave with Mary and Samuel right behind her. In the firelight her shadow loomed large against the darkness of the trees. She took a deep breath, raised the hatchet high above her head, and struck him squarely in the chest.

Moving from slumbering body to body, she struck her hated enemy with his own weapon, the weapon used to raid her house and kill her friends and neighbors. Mary and Samuel were right behind her, striking too, again and again, Mary hesitantly but Samuel swiftly and surely. As blood spattered around them Hannah paused only once, when she looked down and saw that the Indian cowering under her bloodstained tomahawk was not an adult, but a small boy. Enraged as she was, Hannah knew that she could not kill a little child, not even in vengeance for the death of her baby daughter. Her bloody hand frozen in midair, she paused. In that moment the boy ran off into the woods.

When the gruesome business was finished, the little boy and an old woman, who had heard the commotion and managed to escape in time, were the only two Indians left alive. The rest were dead, hacked to death by Hannah, Mary and Samuel, using the Indians' own tomahawks. For a moment there was quiet, the only sounds their breathing and the quiet settling of the fire. But very quickly Hannah realized that they needed to escape the island as soon as possible.

"The boy got away and so did an old woman. We need to get out of here. Come, Mary, get some food. Samuel, you go down and take care of the canoes."

After grabbing some food and taking a tomahawk and a gun, Hannah and Mary scrambled down the bluff to the beach where they saw that Samuel had sunk all of the canoes except one. They looked here and there and could see no signs of life on either shores of the river. The boy and old woman were out there somewhere, but where had they gone? How soon would they find other Indians to help them? Driven by this fear, Hannah, Mary and Samuel jumped into the remaining canoe and quickly began paddling down the Merrimack River.

They had not gone far when Hannah suddenly called to the others to stop. A thought had occurred to her: once they got home, who would believe their story without evidence to prove it? And, if a prize was available for Indian scalps, why shouldn't they claim it? They needed to go back to the island, scalp the Indians they had just killed, and then make their escape. This was a very unexpected decision and immediately raised fear and doubt in Mary's and Samuel's hearts. How could they possibly go back to that place of blood and death? Did they have the strength to make it up the bluffs again? Surely Indians would find them by now and then what? The idea of returning was unthinkable and yet, how could they question the woman who had so boldly masterminded their freedom? How could they possibly refuse her?

Slowly, Samuel turned the canoe around and headed back upstream, afraid of what might lie ahead. Although they said not a word, both he and Mary didn't want to think of what would happen if they were recaptured. But Hannah was resolute and they knew they could not change her mind.

Back on the island Hannah, Mary and Samuel again climbed the bluff and faced the scene they had so recently left behind – dead bodies surrounding the cold ashes of the campfire. Samuel, remembering what the Indian brave had taught him, grabbed one body by the hair and quickly scalped it while the women watched. Then, without a word, all three set to work. When they had scalped all the dead they collected the grisly remains in a large cloth Hannah found nearby. The awful business finished, they hurried back into the canoe and finally headed south, towards home.

The going was treacherous and slow. With Indians everywhere in the woods bordering both sides of the river, they didn't know where to position the canoe so that it was out of sight. Soon it was dawn. They didn't dare to travel by day so they put up in a thicket of underbrush and waited through the long hours until it would be dark again and they could proceed.

Day after day they inched south. Everyday that they eluded capture was a source of quiet relief. Their sense of anticipation grew. But would it be possible to actually get home safely? Just because they had not encountered Indians up to now did not ease their constant fear of being discovered by an enemy who might be lurking behind the trees just around the next bend in the river.

For Hannah anticipation mixed with dread. Now that it looked like they might get home safely, she panicked at the thought of what she would find there. After all she had already been through how could she handle more loss in her life? Would she find Thomas and the children safe? Were they lost to her forever? Had she survived so much only to have to carry on alone?

CHAPTER SIX - THE RETURN

On the last morning, when they knew that they must be close to home, they beached the canoe for good and walked the rest of the way. After what they had been through, the once-familiar trails seemed strange and otherworldly. As soon as they approached the village, they separated: Mary Neff went home to her son and daughter-in-law and Hannah, keeping Samuel close to her side, walked the last mile to where the farm had been on the outskirts of Haverhill.

Her heart was beating hard in her chest and in the years after she always remembered the feelings of dread that refused to be quieted. Could it be? Would they be there?

She heard them before she saw them. With a lurch of her heart she recognized the voice of Thomas, her beloved husband, and at last she knew that he had survived. She ran towards the skeleton of the fire-ravaged house and quickly looked to see if all of the children were there.

"Family! I am here," she called as soon as she and Samuel were within earshot. "I am here, thanks be to God."

"Mother! It is you!" As they rushed to her, the children could hardly believe that before them stood the mother they had known to be dead. And where was the baby? Who was that young man with her? It was almost more than they could grasp.

Later, as they settled back together again, the children's stories tumbled out, first from one and then the other. Excitedly, they told her about the ear-piercing noise that had surrounded them and how their father had suddenly appeared on horseback. His few quick orders had sent them running through snow-covered fields towards the garrison house, about a mile away. Thomas grabbed two-year-old Timothy up on his saddle and rode behind them, urging them on and covering their backs. They had not gone far when shots rang out and the children quickly realized that some Indians were behind them, catching up fast. As the children frantically raced onwards, Thomas reined in the horse, turned and fired back. This gave them just enough time to scramble to safety.

But once inside the stout and heavily fortified house, they had searched for their mother and the new baby, confident that she would have been there. Where was she? It was only afterwards, when the raid was over and the victims identified that the family had finally realized: Hannah, baby Martha and Mary were gone! How costly this Indian raid had been for them!

Hannah's Revenge

Afterwards, Hannah's story - and Martha's - was told, but slowly, with Samuel's help. Now safe again in the warm circle of her family, she could hardly believe all that happened was not just an awful nightmare.

But if Hannah was shy about sharing her tale with her family, she was certainly not shy about what to do now that she was safe at home. After they had left the island and were beginning their flight home she had remembered what she had heard about a bounty given by the General Court of Massachusetts for Indian scalps. That was what had impelled her decision to go back to the island. Now was the time to make good on that plan.

On April 21, 1697, a few weeks after they had returned home, Hannah, Thomas, Mary Neff and Samuel Leonardson went to Boston to tell their story. They took with them not only the scalps, still bundled in the large white linen cloth, but also the gun and tomahawk. Because Hannah as a woman had no legal standing before the court, it was Thomas who presented the petition on her behalf. Unbeknownst to the Dustins, the court had repealed the bounty months before Hannah's capture but, despite that, they voted a generous award of twenty-five pounds for Hannah and twelve pounds, ten shillings each for Mary Neff and Samuel Leonardson.

These were truly magnificent gifts but they were not the only ones to follow. While waiting for the money to be given, Hannah told her story to Rev. Cotton Mather, the well-known Puritan preacher and writer. From there the tale spread like wild fire throughout the colonies.

It was not long before Hannah Dustin found herself the most famous woman in America.

Back home again, gifts, money and visitors began to arrive at the Dustin's farm. One gift that survives to this day is a pewter cup presented by Colonel Nicholson, the governor of the Maryland colony. Most people came directly to the Dustin farm. First it was their neighbors but soon others began to arrive from far and wide. It seemed that it wasn't only Hannah that they wanted to see but also the gun, tomahawk and especially the bloody cloth.

Always the practical one, Hannah took to charging visitors for their chance to see the grisly items. Eventually Hannah, Mary and Samuel faded back into their ordinary lives. But history did not entirely forget Hannah Dustin. In the centuries since, Hannah's story has ridden successive waves of praise and criticism.

More than a hundred years later, two well-known New England writers voiced their opinions on Hannah Dustin.

Henry David Thoreau wrote an admiring account of Hannah, the Indian raid and its aftermath in his "A Week on the Concord and Merrimack Rivers," a travel journal published in 1849. But, writing about the same time, Nathaniel Hawthorne described Hannah as "a bloody old hag," who he wished, "had sunk over head and ears in a swamp, and been there buried, until summoned forth to comfort her victims at the Day of Judgment."

In 1861, there was an attempt to put up a marble statue honoring Hannah Dustin in Haverhill, Massachusetts, but because of the Civil War then raging, the sponsors were unable to come up with the funds and the project was abandoned. In 1874, a large granite statue of Hannah was erected in New Hampshire, on the island where the killings had taken place, now known as Dustin Island. This entire monument, which stands twenty-five feet high, depicts Hannah with a hatchet in her right hand and a bundle of scalps in her left fist. The figure of Hannah herself is seven and half feet tall and shows her with one foot bare, for she was said to have lost a shoe when captured and rushed from her home.

It is believed that Hannah Dustin was the first woman in the United States to have been so honored.

Five years later, in 1879, a second Dustin monument was built in Haverhill. This statue, which also shows Hannah with hatchet in hand, stands in GAR Park in downtown Haverhill.

Nor has controversy about Hannah and her story waned since. There have been articles, both for and against her in the Haverhill press. There are those who have contended that she killed mostly women and children and scalped them for profit. Others have written about the strength and courage it must have taken not only to plan but also execute such a daring escape. It has been noted that during the brutal French and Indian wars, many colonists were taken captive and marched to Canada. A very few escaped; some were ransomed by their families and returned home; some chose to remain in Canada. Most were never heard from again. There exists no other recorded instance of anyone who killed their captives and escaped alive.

It has been written that we should not look at history and judge it by today's standards. We must examine it in its own context. The following, excerpted from a newspaper article by Barney Gallagher on Sept. 10, 2006 in the *The Eagle-Tribune of North Andover, MA,* is noteworthy: "Those were brutal times. The settlers and the Indians were both involved in brutality toward one another…The Indians were defending their territory, and the settlers were defending themselves from the Indians. If there is blame, let it be shared… Let's just understand how things were then, not how things are now."

So, with this understanding we remember and honor Hannah Dustin.

About the Author

Juanita Carey at the Hannah Dustin statue in Boscawen, NH.

Juanita Carey was born in Lima, Peru. She spent her childhood in Lima and in Englewood, New Jersey. She also lived in Europe and various parts of the United States before settling in New Hampshire. After raising her family, Mrs. Carey became a Media Specialist and worked in schools in New York and Ohio. In New Hampshire she served as a Media Generalist and Reading Specialist. The author of articles for newspapers and magazines, Mrs. Carey has also written a biography of the English Bible scholar, E.W. Bullinger. She has five children and thirteen grandchildren, who live in the United States and Europe.